THE ADIRONDACKS:
A Special World

THE ADIRONDACKS:
A Special World

Bill Healy

Published by
North Country Books, Inc.
Utica, New York

At the Railroad Station, Thendara, Herkimer County

THE ADIRONDACKS:
A Special World

by

Bill Healy

First Edition
Copyright © 1986 by Bill Healy
All rights reserved

Library of Congress Cataloging in Publication Data

Healy, Bill, 1952-
The Adirondacks: A Special World

1. Adirondack Mountains (N.Y.) — History.
2. Adirondack Mountains (N.Y.) — Description and travel — Views.
I. Title
F127.A2H648   1985   917.47'53'00222   85-31063
ISBN 0-932052-42-X

———————————————

Published by
North Country Books, Inc.
Utica, New York

Printed and bound in Hong Kong
by Scanner Art Service Inc. Toronto, Canada

Acknowledgements

Like most projects, this book could not have been completed easily without help. Thanks, first and foremost, to my mother, who minded the store while I was out hiking, canoeing, and taking photographs. She also walked a few trails with me, and helped out in many more ways than I can mention. Her assistance and her enthusiasm have meant a lot to me.

Rob Gessner, Kevin Kilrain, and Carl Penk have been my most frequent trail companions over the last few years. We've traveled on foot, skis, snowshoes, and by canoe in every season and in all kinds of weather. My thanks for the company, especially on the trips they would rather forget.

Lou Greppo introduced me to the pleasures of fly fishing in the Adirondacks. Ken Dorn, a fellow book dealer, shared his knowledge of the literature of the region, as well as quite a few stories at late-night talk sessions. His love of the Adirondacks attracts others with similar interests, and the people I've met through him have enriched my knowledge and appreciation of the area.

My wife, Vandra, has given me encouragement through the final stages of the project. I also enjoy introducing her to the area and activities that mean so much to me.

Introduction

The photographs in this volume show the Adirondack mountain region in the 1980s, although many of the views could be pictures of the 1880s, the 1780s, or the 1580s. Parts of the Adirondacks appear as wild today as before man settled the area. Other scenes are different, however, for man has put his mark on the landscape. The wildlife has been hunted, fished, and trapped, the forests lumbered, and the metals and minerals have been mined. Popular with sportsmen and vacationers, the Adirondacks have seen their share of recreational use - and overuse. But rather than destroy the area, man has made an effort to preserve some of its beauty. Today the region is a rather unique state park.

The Adirondacks are not the tallest of mountains; at 5,344 feet, Mount Marcy, the highest, extends little more than a mile above sea level. Tahawus, an alternate name for Marcy, is an Indian word meaning "cloud-splitter," but there are few jagged peaks threatening to tear the sky. Nevertheless, these are real mountains. Rugged and rounded, shaped by uplifts and erosion, carved by glaciers and running water, and containing some of the oldest rock on the face of the earth, today's Adirondacks are the product of more than a billion years of mountain-building. They are attractive mountains, venerable not merely because of their age, but because they have aged well. Solid, with all but the highest peaks clothed in vegetation, the Adirondacks possess a friendly beauty balanced by an awesome ruggedness. Their gray rock, appearing cold on even the sunniest days, reminds one that these mountains have been visited

often - even settled - but never really tamed. Although man has altered the face of the landscape, the mountain rock will outlast us.

The name "Adirondack Mountains" was originally given to only one of the five mountain ranges in northern New York. Ebeneezer Emmons, the state geologist who conducted the first comprehensive survey of the region in 1837 (which included the first ascent and naming of Mount Marcy), wished to commemorate the presence of the Algonquin Indians in the region. Ironically, the word he chose came from the Iroquois, and while there is some question of its true derivation, the most colorful explanation states that it meant "barkeaters," or "those who eat trees." The term was used derisively by the Mohawks to refer to their enemies' dietary practices during periods of economic hardship. Whatever the original meaning, the romantic sound of the name caught the attention of those who heard it, and it was soon applied to the entire area.

The Adirondack Region covers most of the northern portion of New York State, from Lake Champlain to the Saint Lawrence River, and from the Mohawk Valley foothills to the Canadian border. For descriptive purposes, however, the most useful boundary is man-made: the "blue line" drawn on maps to indicate the limits of the Adirondack Park, established by the State Legislature in 1892. These boundaries now enclose approximately six million acres of land, public and private, with a variety of natural features. High peaks, dense forests, woodland ponds, rolling hills, and a vast system of interconnecting lakes, rivers, and streams lie within the

Blue Line. All contribute to the character of the region; we speak of the mountains, but one can find beauty without gazing at high peaks or taking in the views from lofty summits.

The rugged terrain makes the Adirondacks rather inhospitable, and the mountain area was slow to be settled. Permanent residency followed the European discovery of North America; Iroquois and Algonquin tribes traveled through the region, hunted, fished, and fought each other there, but appear to have made no lasting settlements beyond the foothills. The French, English, and Dutch made few efforts to explore or settle the area, despite their interest in the beaver pelts and other furs found there. Indian alliances (and animosities) made in the Adirondacks had a significant bearing on the outcome of the struggle for European control of North America, but the mountains were generally considered an obstacle in the path to more promising land in the west. The first real exploration and settlement came in the late 18th and early 19th centuries.

Most of the land in the Adirondacks was bought and sold before it was explored - in fact, before the mountains were named. Large tracts of land were sold in the late 1700s, usually for pennies an acre, to speculators hoping to profit from the resources of the region. Settlers moved in. Most came from Vermont and other New England states; after trying to farm the land, many turned to hunting and trapping to supplement their incomes. Miners and lumbermen also found their way to the northern New York wilderness. While iron ore was the first attraction, today the region has proved to be an important source of titanium, zinc, lead, talc, garnet, and wollastonite. In addition to lumber for building, Adirondack trees provided charcoal, potash, bark for leather tanning, and wood pulp for papermaking. Lumbering started slowly, but accelerated to such a degree in the late 19th century that one now finds very little virgin timber left.

The first vacationers arrived not long after the early settlers. Most were sportsmen, hunters and fishermen lured by reports of abundant fish and game. Usually business or professional men, they had leisure time for vacations as well as money to indulge in hobbies.

The 19th century was also a time when Americans were developing a new appreciation of wilderness. Most of the eastern wild lands had been tamed, and the majority of the population now lived in cities. Industrialization and urbanization brought new pressures on society. While men still wished to subdue the wilderness to serve the needs of their civilization, there was a growing romantic conception of wilderness as aesthetically pleasing on its own. Thoreau, Emerson, and a few other writers are often cited as spokesmen for the period, but many popular authors of the day voiced similar sentiments. Some visited the Adirondacks, found wilderness and adventure there, and wrote about it.

Charles Fenno Hoffman, John Todd, Joel Tyler Headley, Alfred Billings Street, and S.H. Hammond were among the earliest to publish accounts of their Adirondack adventures. The first to capture a large share of the public's attention, however, was a Boston minister, William Henry Harrison Murray. "Adirondack" Murray's *Adventures in the Wilderness* (Boston, 1869) started a stampede of tourists to the northern woods. A collection of tales perhaps loosely based upon actual experiences, the book was not just entertainment, but an exhortation to visit the Adirondacks. Part travel guide, it told the reader what to bring, how to get there, where to go, what to expect - even *why* one should go. The only problem was that many readers took Murray's words literally. When their experiences failed to live up to their expectations, some felt they had been misled. The disgruntled adventurers became known as "Murray's Fools," but controversy only increased interest in the Adirondacks; thousands came to visit the region every year, and the numbers have increased to millions today.

The Adirondacks became a fashionable resort. Large hotels were built, local residents guided the "sports" who came to hunt and fish, and wealthy visitors purchased land for elaborate camps and estates. It was a time of servants, private railroad cars, and steamboats on Lake George, Racquette Lake, and Blue Mountain Lake. The area also attracted vacationers of more modest means (although not as many as after the introduction of the automobile), as well as thousands of invalids suffering from tuberculosis and other respiratory ailments. Murray and his contemporaries praised the healthful and restorative qualities of Adirondack air and camp life, bringing many in search of magic cures as well as recreation.

The development of a tourist industry revealed a need to protect the wilderness. Vacationers, sportsmen, hotel owners, and guides could see the destruction caused by the lumbermen. It was a time when we still believed that our natural resources were inexhaustable, and the lumber companies had little use for the land after the trees were cut. The land left behind was not only ugly, but susceptible to forest fires which destroyed even more timber. While the lumber industry wielded great power, opposing economic interests also had much at stake. Years of struggle resulted in the creation of the Forest Preserve in 1885 and the Adirondack Park in 1892. Further protection to the state lands and its forests came two years later, when the following words were written into the new State Constitution:

> "The lands of the state, now owned or hereafter acquired, constituting the Forest Preserve as now fixed by law, shall be forever kept as wild forest lands. They shall not be leased, sold or exchanged, or be taken by any corporation, public or private, nor shall the timber thereon be sold, removed, or destroyed."

This "forever wild" clause embodies the spirit of a preservationist philosophy of wilderness protection. The current administration of this philosophy by the Adirondack Park Agency is controversial today, but it gave the region the protection it needed to recover from the devastation of the 19th century. Earlier, less stringent legislation aimed at protecting the forests was too easily circumvented; these unequivocal words will let future generations enjoy the beauty of the Adirondacks. Any relaxation of the laws would allow the abuses of the past to be repeated.

Of course, the lumbermen were not solely responsible for the damage to the region. Sportsmen eliminated much of the wildlife. Game laws were nonexistant or ignored in the last century, and deer were usually taken by hounding or jacklighting, two unsportsmanlike practices outlawed today. Writings of the period often tell of tremendous quantities of deer and trout that were caught and killed, and contemporary photographs all too often sadly confirm the stories. Confusing the quantity of game taken with the quality of the experience, hunters extirpated the moose, elk, and most of the deer. Other predators, such as the wolf, lynx, and panther, were considered nuisances and eliminated by bounty hunters.

Thus, like all wild areas close to human settlements, the Adirondack environment was greatly changed by contact with man. While not suited to agriculture or urban development, the region contains abundant natural resources and great recreational potential. Both were exploited without regard for the consequences until conflicts arose. The creation of the Adirondack Park altered the course of development without stopping it; the land, forests, waters, and wildlife are now protected by law. For those acquainted with the National Park System, it is quite different from our usual concept of a wilderness park. Composed of private as well as public land, it is a park in which people live and work, not just a piece of land set aside for temporary recreational use. Lumbering and mining continue on private land, although usually out of sight of the casual visitor; there are resorts and theme parks for those who take vacations to be entertained. Lake shores are dotted with thousands of private camps, ranging from simple cabins to magnificent rustic estates. One sees ample evidence of the taming of the wilderness, but a short distance from the towns, ski areas, and golf courses lie the Adirondacks in which man is only a visitor - the Adirondacks that are mandated by law to remain "forever wild."

The High Peaks from Vanderwacker Mountain, Essex County

Sacandaga River above Auger Falls, Hamilton County

From the Scenic View on Rte. 30, Sabael, Hamilton County

Dix and Hunter's Pass from Noonmark, Essex County

Cedar River Flow, Hamilton County

On Owl's Head Mountain, Hamilton County

Beaver Dam, Snowy Mountain, Hamilton County

Fall Colors, Lake George Wild Forest Area, Washington County

MacIntyre Brook, High Peaks Wilderness Area, Essex County

Blowdown on Giant Mountain, Essex County

On Second Brother Mountain, Essex County

Hudson River near North Creek, Warren County

Forked Lake, Hamilton County

High Falls on the Oswegatchie River, St. Lawrence County

Near Cascade Pond, Hamilton County

Fall Colors, Lake George Wild Forest Area, Washington County

Racquette River below Buttermilk Falls, Hamilton County

Along the Oswegatchie River, St. Lawrence County

Eckford Chain of Lakes from Blue Mountain, Hamilton County

Marsh along Rte. 30, north of Speculator, Hamilton County

Fish Brook Pond, Lake George Wild Forest Area, Washington County

Payne Brook, along the Northville-Lake Placid Trail, Hamilton County

Giant Mountain from Noonmark, Essex County

33

Sleeping Beauty Mountain, Lake George Wild Forest Area, Washington County

34

Rock Pond near Lake Durant, Hamilton County

From the Three Brothers Trail, Essex County

Bunchberry Plants, Second Brother Mountain, Essex County

Oswegatchie River from High Rock, St. Lawrence County

The High Peaks from Big Slide Mountain, Essex County

Along Rte. 28, Warren County

The Summit of Cascade Mountain, looking north to Whiteface, Essex County

Towards Lake Champlain from Giant Mountain, Essex County

Creek Road, near the Town of Hope, Hamilton County

Exploring the Adirondacks

"It makes a man feel what it is to have all creation under his feet. There are woods there which it would take a lifetime to hunt over, mountains that seem shouldering each other to boost the one whereon you stand, up and away Heaven knows where. Thousands of little lakes are let in among them so light and clean. Old Champlain, though fifty miles away, glistens below you like a strip of white birch when slicked up by the moon on a frosty night, and the Green Mountains of Vermont beyond it fade and fade away until they disappear as gradually as a cold scent when the dew rises."

So, we are told, spoke guide John Cheney of the view from the summit of Mount Marcy. Cheney's rustic, yet eloquent comments may have been polished by Charles Fenno Hoffman for publication in his *Wild Scenes in the Forest and Prairie* (London, 1839), but there should be little doubt that his sentiments were accurately captured. The range of topography, the breadth of the views, and the wild appearance of the landscape remain impressive. In terms of size, the 9,375 square miles within the Blue Line make Adirondack Park the largest in the contiguous United States.

It is a big area to explore. In his *Adirondack Country* (New York, 1954), William Chapman White states, "No one, with the exception of state surveyors and the Conservation Department pilots, knows all of it." I doubt that they could claim to have a detailed knowledge of the entire area. Although roads now cross the Park in every direction, a glance at a map shows that much of the land is still accessible only to those who travel by foot or boat. Six million

acres, traversed in that manner, takes a long time to cover - and a lot longer to know. The ability to recognize landmarks is not enough; one must become familiar with the landscape, the wildlife, and every aspect of the environment, following their changes through the seasons. As Longstreth said in his book, *The Adirondacks* (New York, 1917), "to know the region intimately, to know where you will find the trout, where you will see the deer, where the berries grow, to recognize the mountains as you would friends, takes years."

Lumbering and mining are important to the region, but most people come to the Adirondacks for recreation. The State of New York owns 2.3 million acres of land within the Blue Line, and it is open to the public for activities such as boating, hiking, camping, hunting, and fishing. The Adirondack Park Agency has established land use classifications and regulations to preserve some of the wilderness character of the region, but generally visitors are allowed a great deal of freedom on public land. With only a few restrictions, one can camp for brief periods on state land throughout the Park; those with a craving for adventure can sample all the wildness the Adirondacks have to offer.

Whether one comes to camp or stay at a resort, the scenic beauty of the landscape is a primary attraction. Yet the wild areas are not vast; in fact, it is difficult to find a spot more than a day's walk from a highway or settlement. However, one need not travel far from the roads to find wilderness, for the dense forests muffle man-made noises a short distance from their sources, and within minutes of leaving a trailhead, often the only evidence of man is the path through the woods, or perhaps the vestiges of lumbering or mining activity which took place decades earlier. Not all areas are so unspoiled, but nature has made great progress in obscuring evidence of past human use.

The simplest (and to my mind the most satisfying) way to explore the Adirondacks is by walking. There are hundreds of miles of foot trails suitable for day hikes or longer journeys in every section of the Park. On the most elementary level, little more is needed than a good pair of sneakers or walking shoes, and perhaps a small pack to hold lunch and a windbreaker or sweater. More elaborate equipment is required as one becomes more ambitious, or when planning to stay overnight. Difficult conditions and unexpected weather changes can be encountered at any time of the year, so it is no place to play at having a "wilderness experience." While distances are not great, help is far away when an emergency arises, and individuals or groups in remote areas must rely on their own resources. Proper preparation is essential to enjoying the pleasures of hiking to mountain peaks, remote streams and ponds, and other secluded spots in the Adirondack backcountry.

Those who crave views from lofty summits usually head for the High Peaks Region, located in the northeast sector of the Park near the hamlets of Lake Placid and Keene Valley. This area contains all of the Adirondack peaks over 4,000 feet in height; forty-six are officially recognized, although recent measurements have amended the count to forty-two. They have been the focus of hikers' attention since Robert and George Marshall and Herbert Clark became the first to climb all forty-six in the 1920s. By the mid-1930s, a club had been formed by others who had duplicated their feat, and membership in the "Forty-Sixers" now approaches 2,000. Slightly over half of these peaks have one or more trails to their summits, while the rest have informal paths which most hikers follow to minimize erosion. The views from many of these mountains are quite spectacular, not only of the surrounding High Peaks, but also of lesser

mountains, lakes, and the narrow passes which appear to have been cut between the mountains with a knife. While one need not climb all forty-six, a look from at least one is essential to gaining a complete perspective of this section of the Park.

Mount Marcy receives many visitors, often simply because it is the highest mountain in the Adirondacks (and the state). It is the only summit from which all forty-six High Peaks can be seen, although Longstreth characterized it as "a view of a stupendous jumble . . . like being on top of the biggest bubble in a boiling cauldron." Nevertheless, one cannot help being impressed looking *down* at mountains which are so imposing when viewed from lower elevations, and there is satisfaction in knowing that one cannot climb any higher. Of course, the nearby peaks offer different but equally fine views. Giant Mountain provides a panorama of the High Peaks, and the Ridge Trail from Chapel Pond rewards the hiker with ever-widening views of the surrounding mountains as one climbs to the summit. Big Slide gives a sweeping view of Marcy and the Great Range, set off by the steep rock face which gives the mountain its name. Haystack was rated by the Marshalls as having the best view of all the High Peaks. Several of the mountains under 4,000 feet also afford fine views, notably Noonmark, Pitchoff Mountain, Mount Jo, and the Three Brothers (whose trail is also an excellent route to Big Slide Mountain from Keene Valley). A walk through a mountain pass completes any picture of the High Peaks; the trail through Avalanche Pass, for example, leads one through dense forests nestled between steep cliffs, giving the hiker a taste of the wildness that has always been an impediment to travelers in the region.

Bigger mountains are not necessarily better, however. The view from Cathead Mountain, in southern Hamilton county near Benson, shows rugged, forested mountains that rival the largest, despite altitudes which rarely approach 3,000 feet. To the east, Lake George is bordered by mountains, the Tongue Mountain Range (one of the few places in the Park where rattlesnakes are found) on the western side, with Buck Mountain, Shelving Rock,

Erebus, Black Mountain, and others on the eastern shore. Near Indian Lake, 3,899-foot Snowy Mountain looms over Indian and Lewey Lakes, while Blue Mountain to the north exhibits a commanding presence in the lake country of the central Adirondacks. From its summit one can see the Eckford Chain, Racquette Lake, Forked Lake, Long Lake, and on a clear day, the High Peaks to the northeast. Because of their lower base elevations, a number of these mountains have a greater vertical rise than many 4,000-foot peaks.

The southern, central, and western areas of the Adirondacks offer more than mountains. The ponds, lakes, and streams are favorites of fishermen, as well as of hikers whose interests extend beyond "peak-bagging." There are extensive trail networks in the Pharoah Lakes Wilderness Area and the Lake George Wild Forest Area, where one can visit more bodies of water than mountain peaks. The West Canada Lakes region, once the home of French Louie Seymour, the hermit, is almost as wild and inaccessible now as in the days when he set his traps through the woods. Many trails follow old logging roads, as well as a few currently used by lumber companies where trails briefly cross private land. Although most of these areas were heavily lumbered, there are still a few stands of virgin timber tucked away, and there has been much new growth since timber harvesting ceased on land owned by the state. It is a different world from the High Peaks; the mountains offer challenging climbs, but one can spend years exploring without ascending to a single summit, enjoying the splendor of the woods and waters.

Water is an integral part of the Adirondack landscape. Many of the hundreds of lakes and ponds are linked by rivers and streams, or separated by only short land distances, allowing extended trips between these bodies of water - if one has the right kind of boat.

The canoe is the traditional North American wilderness watercraft, but Adirondack guides developed a new vessel suited to their particular needs called (appropriately enough) the "Adirondack guide-boat." Double-ended, and rowed rather than paddled, the guide-boat was highly maneuverable for hunting and fishing with passengers, yet light enough to be transported by the guide alone over the "carries." Its use declined as the employment of guides waned in the early 20th century, but there is currently a revival of interest in this unique indigenous craft. Many original guide-boats have been restored, and present-day makers are constructing new boats, in the traditional manner as well as of modern materials such as fiberglass. The canoe and guide-boat are well suited to the quiet exploration of the lakes and winding rivers of the Adirondacks. For those who desire more action in their adventures, the Hudson, Black, Sacandaga, and Salmon Rivers are noted for their stretches of rapids, which are run in canoes, kayaks, and ever-increasing numbers of inflatable boats.

Adirondack waterways have been heavily used since the early 19th century. While the private ownership of some land has closed a few routes, many of the most popular ones remain open. The best known canoe trail begins at Old Forge with the Fulton Chain, and from Racquette Lake either heads up the Marion River to Blue Mountain Lake, or along the Racquette River through Forked Lake, Long Lake, and on to the Saranacs or Tupper Lake. The large hotels once found along the route are now gone, but the shores are still lined with camps. The Marion River Carry from Utowana Lake, following what was once the roadbed of the world's shortest standard gauge railroad, and the "Great Camps," such as William West Durant's Camp Pine Knot on Racquette Lake, recall an era of rustic elegance in the latter part of the 19th century. That period is now part of the past, and nature is quickly reclaiming the land. Some sections of these routes are more wild today than a century ago.

Other water trails take one away from the populated areas. The Saint Regis Canoe Area offers all the wilderness that one is willing to paddle and carry a canoe to reach. The Oswegatchie River from Inlet to High Falls (and beyond) is a beautiful winding wilderness tour, with little evidence of man besides the leantos, campsites, and other people one passes along the route. It is one of the wildest parts of the Adirondack Park today, even though there have been lumber camps and a resort at High Falls in the past. Countless streams and small rivers offer short stretches of wilderness, often of only a few miles. The feeling of wildness comes quickly, however, for the Adirondacks are not known so much for unbroken stretches of wilderness as for having pockets of truly wild country amid roads and settlements.

Those who lack the time or inclination to travel into the backcountry can find many sights worth seeing along the highways. The introduction of the automobile opened the Adirondacks to more people than ever before, and led to the development of the roads which now make every part of the region accessible to travelers. Trips along routes 28, 30, 9N, 73, and other major highways expose one to a wide range of scenery, and side roads offer more intimate views to those who take the time to explore them. One can drive to the summits of two Adirondack peaks, Whiteface Mountain near Elizabethtown and Prospect Mountain near Lake George. Sights can pass too quickly if one drives without stopping, of course, but the scenery viewed through a car window should not be underestimated. Roads pass through some of the most beautiful sections of the Park.

Modern highways have put the region within a day's drive of millions of people in the northeastern United States. Many living outside the Blue Line can reach the Adirondacks in two hours or less; with an early start, one can have a full day of activities and return home for the night. Mountains can be climbed, trails walked, lakes and rivers can be paddled, sailed, or cruised. There is ample time for fishing, hunting, skiing, picnicking, and sightseeing. One can spend years exploring the Adirondacks piece by piece, one day at a time.

Sometimes, however, one needs a little longer. A good way to experience the wildness of the Adirondacks is by spending a night or two. A sunset, the cry of a loon, the crackle and smell of a campfire, or a nocturnal visit from local wildlife (anything from a chipmunk to a black bear) are missed by those who take only day trips. While a fire can warm a cabin or lodge, the best place for one is out-of-doors. Cars can be driven right up to tent sites in state and private campgrounds, but one can find more solitude in the wilderness areas and state campsites which are accessible only by boat. The state provides leantos along many trails and water routes, although veteran campers usually carry a tent, since unoccupied leantos are now a rare commodity. Even suitable wilderness campsites are difficult to find in areas such as the High Peaks on holiday weekends, which suggests that those who come to the Adirondacks for peace and quiet should find other times to visit.

The early vacationers usually came only during the warmer months, but today the seasons rarely restrict outdoor activity. Spring and fall attract visitors for the wildflowers and foliage, and winter is a special world in itself. The snow-covered ground can be traveled on skis or snowshoes, and with the proper equipment no spot is unreachable. Cold weather travel requires greater care and planning than other times, since minor accidents can quickly become life-threatening situations, but the rewards are great. The woods are never so silent, or the skies more blue and clear. The trails provide a smooth walking surface when packed with snow, and one's footsteps are erased with the spring thaw. Black flies, the curse of the Adirondacks in spring and early summer, mosquitoes, and other biting insects are absent. There are also fewer people about, so it is one of the best times to enjoy the solitude of the wilderness. However, one can enjoy the mountains, lakes, and forests in any season - except, perhaps, the hunting season, when the prudent hiker usually stays out of the woods.

The variety of natural features which make up the Adirondack landscape offer possibilities for many activities. Besides trails for the hiker, there are steep rock faces that challenge experienced mountain climbers. There are lakes and flat-water rivers for boaters, as well as some of the wildest rapids in the eastern United States for the whitewater enthusiast. Ausable Chasm in Essex County, High Falls Gorge near Wilmington, and Natural Stone Bridge and Caves at Pottersville are commercial "scenic attractions;" no longer part of the wilderness, these areas have lost none of their wild beauty. Tour boats cruise the waters of Lake George, and one can take summer and fall chairlift rides at several ski areas. There are many ways to explore the Adirondacks.

The best part of many of these activities is that they offer one a taste of adventure. Although there are risks and responsibilities associated with wilderness travel, the fact that you are on your own in the Adirondacks is also an attraction. There are mountains with highways to their summits, and roadside turnoffs with inspiring views, but it is also fitting that some sights should be a reward for an expenditure of energy. Like the earliest vacationers in the 19th century, many come to the area today to get away from other people, to enjoy the peace and solitude of the lakes and mountains. The fact that quiet moments and secluded places (as well as the opportunity for real wilderness adventure) can be found so close to millions of people is truly amazing - and a comfort to those who have discovered that the Adirondack Region is a special world.

Beaver House on the Kunjamuk River, Near Speculator, Hamilton County

Thirteenth Lake, Warren County

The Outlet of Lewey Lake, Hamilton County

Keene Valley from Noonmark, Essex County

The Summit of Mount Marcy, Essex County

Trail on Second Brother Mountain, Essex County

Along Rte. 73 near Chapel Pond Pass, Essex County

Trailside, Snowy Mountain, Hamilton County

The Trail to Hadley Mountain, Saratoga County

East Stoney Creek, Hamilton County

Johns Brook, Essex County

Towards Algonquin from Cascade Mountain, Essex County

Trail to Murphy Lake, Hamilton County

63

Oak Mountain from the Sacandaga River near Speculator, Hamilton County

Approaching the Summit of Cascade Mountain, Essex County

View along the Ridge on Giant Mountain towards Dix Mountain, Essex County

The Edge of a Pond, Spruce Mountain, Saratoga County

The Giant's Washbowl, Giant Mountain Wilderness Area, Essex County

Elk Lake from Macomb Mountain, Essex County

Glen Creek, Warren County

Lewey Lake Outlet, Hamilton County

Buttermilk Falls, Hamilton County

Trail, Lake George Wild Forest Area, Washington County

74

Auger Falls, near Wells, Hamilton County

A Stream on Snowy Mountain, Hamilton County

Oswegatchie River at High Rock, St. Lawrence County

Young Bullhead Catfish in Fish Brook Pond, Washington County

Fall Colors along Rte. 30, Franklin County

Indian Lake from Snowy Mountain, Hamilton County

Lake Clear Outlet, Whiteface Mountain in the distance, Franklin County

Descending the Ridge Trail, Giant Mountain, Essex County

Tirrell Pond and the High Peaks from Blue Mountain, Hamilton County

Down the Trail on Phelps Mountain, Algonquin and Wright Peak in the distance, Essex County

Living In The Adirondacks

The uniqueness of the Adirondack Park lies in the fact that it is composed of both public and private land. The constant trumpeting of the phrase "forever wild" sometimes obscures the fact that the region is inhabited. People go about their daily business in these mountains. The visitor sees wildness as an aspect of the beauty of the region; residents may see that, too, but they also see it as a factor to be overcome in order to survive. Resources must be exploited in order for people to make a living. The protection given to state land by the law locks up many of the resources, but private property within the Blue Line is open to commercial use.

Although settlements are found in every part of the Park, the region is not heavily populated. At the time of the last census, slightly fewer than 120,000 persons were living within the Park boundaries - less than fifteen per square mile. A significant portion of these permanent residents are either older adults or children, since younger adults seeking steady jobs and careers are often forced to find their fortunes elsewhere. The region's relative isolation and sparse population do not attract many new industries; consequently, the ways of making a living are few, and many are not much different from those of a century ago.

There are many towns and villages within the Blue Line, but no cities; many have only a few hundred residents, and none more than a few thousand. Although the region was avoided by most settlers during America's westward expansion, small groups began to move into the Northern Wilderness after the Revolutionary War. Those who came to farm found the land even less suitable than the rocky New England soil they had left, but many stayed on to forge a living in the mountains. Farm production was supplemented by hunting and trapping, and by the mid-19th century many local residents were employed in lumbering and mining. When tourists began to arrive, people became hotel-keepers or used their knowledge of woodcraft to guide the city vacationers through the unmapped Adirondack forests. It was necessary to possess a variety of skills in order to make a living, although even that did not guarantee economic security. It did make the people hardy and self-reliant, however, essential qualities for those who wish to live in the Adirondacks year-round.

How do people make a living in the Adirondacks? It is not an easy proposition, and never has been. A few small farms still exist, lumbering and mining continue on private land, and the trapping of fur-bearing animals continues to provide a supplemental income for some families. Recreation and tourism make up a large part of the Adirondack economy; people operate and work at motels and resorts, recreation complexes, and in wilderness activities. It is dependent upon the millions of vacationers who visit the region every year, and thus is affected by such diverse factors as the weather and the national economy, but it is still the area's biggest business. If scenery can be considered a natural resource (and many would argue that it is an important but intangible one), then all commercial activities in the Adirondack Region are an exploitation of its natural resources.

Vacationers are not likely to realize the extent of mining activity in the Adirondacks today, since little evidence is seen from the highways. The region supplies a variety of materials to national and world markets, and its resources are of great importance. The Barton Garnet Mine at North Creek is the world's largest, supplying over 90% of the world's industrial garnet. The nation's largest zinc mine is located at Balmat, and the largest open pit magnetite mine in the world is at Star Lake. N. L. Industries' Tahawus Mine is the world's biggest ilmenite operation, and a major supplier of titanium oxide, which is used as a white pigment in paint. The Cabot Corporation's wollastonite mine at Willsboro is also the largest in the world, and Saint Lawrence County is a major supplier of high-quality talc. Other minerals and materials are extracted in smaller quantities. Although Adirondack mines do not employ large numbers of people, they do offer stable and relatively steady employment, since these resources are likely to be in demand on the world market for many years to come.

Overzealous lumbering was detrimental to Adirondack forests in the 1800s, and the major impetus behind the establishment of the Forest Preserve and the Adirondack Park. Trees on Forest Preserve land cannot be legally removed, but those on private land inside the Blue Line can be cut. The lumber companies which own land in the Park harvest both hardwoods and softwoods for lumber, veneer, and paper pulp. The forests are still recovering from the devastation of the past, so the area is no longer a major supplier of wood and wood products, but there is potential for growth in the future. The scientific management of lumber company land provides replacements for trees which are removed, as well as faster growth of the trees to the proper cutting size. In fact, proponents of conservation rather than preservation in wilderness management contend that the forests on managed land are actually "healthier" than those on unmanaged land (specifically, the state land in the Forest Preserve).

The days of the backwoods live-in lumber camps are now gone, as lumbering and mining have become mechanized, but the lumber industry does provide fairly steady employment. People work not only in timber harvesting, but also in sawmills and pulp mills. Besides providing jobs, lumber companies contribute to the local economies by purchasing or leasing timber rights to privately owned land. In turn, many companies lease some of their land to sportsmen's groups for hunting and outdoor recreation, which stimulates the tourism-related aspects of local commerce.

Adirondack residents found ways to earn all or part of a living attending to the needs of early visitors, and over the years tourism has grown into one of the most important components of the region's economy. Knowledge of the mountains and woodcraft made men into valued guides for sportsmen and explorers. Informal offerings of lodging and meals led others to open hotels and eventually resorts. While outsiders developed the commercial establishments more extensively, local residents remained the backbone of the industry which sprang up to serve the needs of the thousands of vacationers that swarmed to the Adirondacks after reading of the adventures of Joel Tyler Headley, Alfred Billings Street, and William Henry Harrison Murray.

Guides were considered essential to anyone traveling the back woods in the middle of the 19th century. Few maps were available, and those that were lacked detail, so outsiders had to rely on the knowledge of the local residents. To the sportsman, the guide was not only well versed in the habits of fish and game, but also a colorful character who added charm to the rustic vacation. Guides entertained their clients as well as worked for them, and the best guides often became trusted friends of their patrons over the years. They became the subjects of stories and legends as they infused the Adirondack experience with their personalities.

But times changed. As roads cut through the region and the mountains were surveyed, the Adirondacks became more accessible and less mysterious. In the 1870s, the writings of George Washington Sears (who published articles in "Forest and Stream" under the pen name "Nessmuk") preached the virtues of light-weight backwoods travel without a guide as the means to achieve a true wilderness experience. Vacationers driving their cars to the Adirondacks in the early 20th century were usually independent people, rarely requiring a guide's assistance. Their ranks dwindled as the demand decreased, although the best known usually found a market for their skills. However, the future of tourism seemed to lie in the development of facilities for activities other than hunting and fishing.

Winter sports were introduced at the Lake Placid Club in the early 1900s and were quite successful. The fact that the Winter Olympics have been held at Lake Placid in 1932 and 1980 is sufficient testimony to the suitability of the region for winter recreation. There are now ski areas (both alpine and cross-country) throughout the Adirondacks, and Lake Placid boasts world class bobsledding, ski jumping, and ice skating facilities. For the warmer seasons, there are marinas on large lakes, and several amusement parks within the Blue Line. The tourist industry has changed and adapted to the times. Places such as Lake George Village are no longer rustic hamlets, but typical of the neon-lighted resort towns found elsewhere. For better or worse, there is something for just about any taste in the Park today, from lavish commercial resorts to video arcades to unspoiled wilderness.

The current interest in wilderness recreation has fostered a revival of the Adirondack guide. While the typical 19th century guide usually took his "sports" on hunting and fishing trips, today's guide is more likely to take his (or her) patrons out for hiking, canoeing, horseback riding, cross-country skiing, or whitewater rafting. And the guides may not always be Adirondack natives - many have moved there from outside the Park, finding that the region offers a perfect environment for the career and lifestyle they wish to pursue.

The large influx of summer tourists has also created a suitable setting for another group - artists and craftspeople. Small Adirondack towns offer a peaceful and attractive place for painters, photographers, woodworkers and furniture makers, boatbuilders, and other artisans to work. Sales of their wares provide personal income and support the local economy. Again, not all are natives, but they have become part of the environment, providing services that visitors expect to see.

Nevertheless, making a living in the Adirondacks is not easy. Incomes are low, among the lowest in the state, and unemployment is high in some seasons. Available jobs rarely require a high degree of skill, and wages are appropriately low. The exploitation of natural resources in lumbering and mining, while providing stable employment, does not require many workers, since machines have replaced much of the human labor needed in the past.

Tourism provides more employment, but the needs are seasonal and constantly fluctuating. Bad weather, a sluggish economy, or a gas shortage can seriously affect the amount of business a resort, ski area, or other establishment does from one year to the next. Yet recreation, which is dependent upon the Adirondack scenery protected by the "forever wild" clause in the State Constitution, contributes a significant amount of income to the region's economy. More tourism would mean greater income, but since the Adirondack area is a state park, the commercial development of private land is subject to strict controls. The regulations are controversial; many residents contend that the Adirondack Park Agency's rules prevent development which would benefit the economy, but on the other hand, the restrictions also help to preserve the beauty that has attracted millions to the lakes and mountains for over a century.

The balance - such as it is - that exists between business interests and wilderness in the Adirondacks can make life hard, but life is hard in any mountain region. Such areas are always out of the paths of commerce. Winter, which means skiing and other winter sports to those outside the region, brings a period of fewer jobs and restricted activities to local residents. Persons living outside the Park who value its wilderness and recreational opportunities should realize the resourcefulness required of those who make their homes within the Blue Line. There should be little wonder that restrictions on development are sometimes met with resistance from local people. But as tough as it is to live there, most residents would probably not trade it for anything else.

View from the Ridge Trail, Giant Mountain, Essex County

The Fire Tower on Hadley Mountain, Saratoga County

The Sacandaga River above Northville, Hamilton County

Cruise Ship Mohican, *Lake George, Warren County*

Black Mountain Pond, Lake George Wild Forest Area,
Washington County

93

Sacandaga River near the Town of Hope, Hamilton County

Ice Fishing on the Great Sacandaga Lake, Fulton County

The Lake Placid Club across Mirror Lake, Essex County

Adirondack Museum, Blue Mountain Lake, Hamilton County

Indian Lake, Hamilton County

Long Lake, Hamilton County

Gore Mountain Ski Center, Warren County

Recovering from 44" of Snow, Warrensburg, Warren County

Olympic Ski Jump near Lake Placid, Essex County

The Sacandaga River at Wells, Hamilton County

At Thirteenth Lake, Warren County

Middle Lake, Hamilton County

Float Plane on Long Lake, Hamilton County

Lake George from Sleeping Beauty Mountain, Washington County

Batchellerville Bridge over Great Sacandaga Lake, Saratoga County

Railroad Station, North Creek, Warren County

The Sagamore Hotel, Bolton Landing, Warren County

Dix Mountain from Noonmark, Essex County

Abandoned Ranger's Cabin,
Goodnow Mountain, Essex County

Abandoned Ranger's Cabin, Snowy Mountain, Hamilton County

Entering Blue Mountain Lake from Eagle Lake, Hamilton County

Mount Marcy from Phelps Mountain, Essex County

Mount Colden from Phelps Mountain, Essex County

116

Front Porch of the Main Lodge, Sagamore Lodge and Conference Center,
Racquette Lake, Hamilton County

117

Blue Mountain Lake from the Adirondack Museum, Hamilton County

Sagamore Lake from Sagamore Lodge, Hamilton County

From the Beach at Old Forge, Herkimer County

At the Railroad Station, Thendara, Herkimer County

A Few Final Words

There is much about the Adirondack Region that cannot be captured on film. The feeling of sitting alone on a 4,000-foot peak, with no one in sight, knowing that no matter how many people have ascended it before, or how many others will follow, you are the only person who has climbed it that day. The canoeist's anticipation of what lies around the bend in a river. The thrill of catching a wild brook trout - and letting it go. The sight of a deer, which still excites me, regardless of how many I've seen. No photograph seems to do justice to the animal.

The two volumes of the *Adirondack Bibliography* list more than 10,000 works concerning the region published up to 1965. The number of books and articles written since that time is not merely large, but massive, keeping pace with the current interest in the area. Faced with this plethora of words, it is sometimes difficult to decide if one is saying anything that hasn't been said before - so I haven't tried. The previous chapters provide only a brief sketch of the region and its history; those who desire more information are encouraged to seek it out. The writings of Alfred L. Donaldson, William Chapman White, Adirondack Murray, and others are readily available, as are books about the Durants and their camps, Noah John Rondeau and French Louie Seymour, and the other people, places, and events that have shaped Adirondack history.

Our appreciation of a subject usually increases as we acquire more knowledge of it. One can enjoy the Adirondacks without studying its natural history, but a little information on the habits and habitats of the plant and animal life can make a view of nature more than just a pretty scene. Similarly, while I enjoyed my first climb up Giant Mountain, that pleasure was enhanced by reading T. Morris Longstreth's account of his experience more than fifty years earlier, and further increased when I learned that Giant was the first peak over 4,000 feet to be climbed in the Adirondacks.

The human history of the region is as important as its natural history. Man has had a great effect on the Adirondack wilderness: he exploited and developed it, almost destroyed it, and ultimately saved it, preserving its beauty for the enjoyment of future generations. The photographs of Seneca Ray Stoddard and other late 19th and early 20th century photographers show scenes of rugged mountains and tranquil lakes, but they also point out some of the damage caused by lumbering activity. The appearance of the landscape would be far different today if it was not for the vision of men who saw that wildness was the greatest natural resource of all.

The region still has its problems for the future. Some say that the Adirondack Park is too successful, that excessive recreational use is taking its toll on the land. Campsites, day use areas, and lakes are often overcrowded. Resort towns teem with tourists - good for the economy, perhaps, but the neon signs and video arcades take away some of the rustic charm that was once part of an Adirondack vacation.

Such use is to be expected, but traffic is also getting heavy in more remote areas. Climbing Cascade Mountain in March, a friend and I were two of eighteen people who signed the trail register bound for the peak that day. Not everyone was on top at once, but we were one of several groups on the summit - a surprise in winter, even if it was a nice day. When another companion and I set up our camp at High Falls on the Oswegatchie River, we found ourselves in the vicinity of more than a score of other campers, including one couple with a portable television. Even after hearing that the Van Hoevenberg Trail to Mount Marcy is often "as crowded as 42nd Street," I was not prepared for the hundreds of people I encountered along the trail and on the summit. So much for the wilderness experience.

It is increasingly difficult (although not impossible) to spend a day alone in the woods without running into others trying to do the same thing. Excessive or careless use, even by those who profess to love the Adirondacks most, has threatened the fragile alpine vegetation on the highest mountain peaks, as well as hastened erosion of the trails and hillsides. The quality of all drinking water is now suspect, and garbage turns up at campsites, leantos, and too many other places.

Is all this recreational use bad? In the west, we hear writer Edward Abbey ranting and raving (and rightfully so) that Americans are too lazy to climb out of their cars to walk around the National Parks. People are doing just that in the Adirondack Park, and they are enjoying it. The Park has the best and most extensive network of trails and waterways of its kind; it is a tribute to the area and to the people that they are well used. The harm comes when people fail to take out their trash - if you carry it in, carry it out.

Robert Marshall, an early lover of the Adirondacks (one of the original "forty-sixers") who went on to become a spokesman for wilderness everywhere, argued that some wild places should be closed to man forever. Suggestions for dealing with the problem of excessive recreational use include hiking permits, quotas, and even competency tests in wilderness skills. All are unacceptable; along with wilderness should be the freedom to enjoy it. I like to be able to go into the Adirondacks where I want and when I want, even on a moment's notice if I suddenly find myself with free time. Crowded conditions will eventually force people to change their activity pat-

terns. I enjoy going out in winter, and spring is nice in spite of - or perhaps because of - the black flies which keep many people away. One must walk and act responsibly, too. While I sometimes cringe when walking on heavily eroded trails, I usually try to stay on them, preferring to let the other areas remain wild and free of my footprints.

The most serious threat to the Adirondacks today comes from the outside, in the form of acid precipitation. Airborne pollution from factories and power plants in the midwest, carried by air currents to the northeast, changes the rain and snow which falls on the area from neutral water to an acid. This precipitation lowers the pH level of the lakes and streams, leaches metals and minerals from the rocks and soil, and generally diminishes the ability of the waters to support life. Only a small percentage of the water bodies in the region are seriously affected at the present time, but the problem is growing. It has become an international issue, and the solution lies outside the Blue Line. Despite some remarks to the contrary, there is overwhelming evidence that industrial pollution is to blame for acid precipitation, that it does present a threat to wildlife and ultimately to ourselves, and that the dollar cost of prevention and cleanup will be far lower and more effective now than later. We are still sometimes rather complacent about the environmental consequences of our actions until it is too late; the Adirondacks were saved once at the end of the last century, but it is up to us to ensure that the phrase "forever wild" has any meaning for the future.

Other problems include the regulation of commerce and development within the Blue Line, and the authority of the Adirondack Park Agency to control it. The local standard of living is not high, and residents are naturally distrustful of any agency that they feel is preventing them from raising it. On the other hand, the entire area is a state park, and public land is mandated by law to remain wild. Development on private land can affect the wildness of adjacent state land; it also seems logical that the authority to oversee all the land within the park boundaries be given to one agency. The area is large enough to support many people engaging in different activities if each uses the land responsibly. People with differing interests in the Adirondacks often seem to be at odds with each other, but it should be possible to accommodate the needs of everyone who wishes to spend time there.

If the photographs and text seem to emphasize wild areas and wilderness activities, it is because they are my personal preferences. Beautiful scenery can be seen without leaving your car, but anyone who has the opportunity to get away from the highways and chooses not to do so is missing something. Many of these photographs were taken on day or overnight trips; they show places which, with a little effort, almost everyone is capable of visiting. There are fine views in every part of the Park, not just in the exotic and hard-to-reach places, although we often overlook the subtle beauties of the things that are right in front of us.

I think that the wilderness areas can be explored and enjoyed best on foot, or in a self-propelled boat such as a canoe or guide-boat. You travel at the right pace to observe the scenery, and by traveling quietly you do not intrude upon the landscape or frighten the animals. After meeting a trapper on a snowmobile while cross-country skiing, I will concede that motorized vehicles have made life much easier for those who must make their living in the Adirondacks, but motors are usually too noisy for my tastes. And besides, I need the exercise.

We usually think of wilderness areas as being vast, remote, and inaccessible. The Adirondacks exhibit only the first of these characteristics, yet the uninhabited areas show many of the qualities of true wildness. Life goes on without much regard for man and his activities. It is a fragile wilderness; because of its proximity to a large human population, it can be quickly and easily eliminated by accident or design. Unlike the remote areas of the world, the Adirondack Mountains are wild because man allows them to be. The mountains are rugged and will outlast us, but we control the look of the landscape. We can let nature take its course, or eliminate any or all wildlife inside the Blue Line. We have seen the effects of uncontrolled and irresponsible lumbering. Although mining never had the same environmental impact, most current operations show little regard for aesthetic considerations when conducting their activities. We are beginning to see the effects of massive recreational use, and the region is seriously treatened by outside pollution in the form of acid precipitation. The land should be used and enjoyed, but it must be used responsibly to ensure that the views we see today will be there for others in the future - or for us when we return.

Like the earliest vacationers in the 19th century, many are drawn to the Adirondacks today by the concept of "forever wild," the idea of a place not under man's domination. There is ample room and opportunity for recreation and adventure; for a day, a week, or for years. One can enjoy the sights through photographs, but it is better to visit, and for that reason there are many scenes that I did not try to capture on film. More than once I set up my camera, composed the scene, set the exposure, and focused, only to decide not to release the shutter. Some views should be enjoyed for the moment, and preserved only in memory, by those who take the time to look for them.

Notes On The Photography

All of the photographs in this book were taken on 35mm transparency film. The use of 35mm equipment allows one to carry a generous amount of camera gear and film with minimum weight and bulk, which is essential when everything is transported on your back. There are always other items one must carry that are not concerned with photography - extra clothes, lunch, maps, first aid kit, etc. Even more on overnight trips. Thus the frequently-heard advice to "keep it simple" has merit. It makes travel easier, and less equipment means that one can concentrate on taking pictures rather than worrying about which gadgets to use. Any extra space in my pack is usually filled with film. You can always manage to take photographs with whatever equipment you have, but not without film. And you can never have enough.

I use both single lens reflex and rangefinder cameras; SLRs offer greater versatility with reflex viewing and interchangeable bodies and lenses, but I also carry a small rangefinder camera for use in inclement weather, or for when I want to travel light and keep things simple. I prefer manual cameras, since they are rugged, dependable, and fully operable with or without batteries, which is desirable when working under the adverse conditions one encounters in winter. I carry lenses of various single focal lengths from 20mm to 200mm, as well as a 2X teleconverter. A tripod is employed whenever possible, and on many occasions when I do not take the time to use one, often compromise by using a monopod. It allows a reasonable degree of camera steadiness at shutter speeds of 1/30 and 1/15 of a second, which I usually use to photograph moving water.

My favorite films are Kodachrome 64 and Fujichrome 100; Kodachrome because of its fine grain and universal acceptance, Fujichrome for its extra speed and because I prefer its color rendition. Some of these photographs were taken on other films by Kodak, Fuji, 3M, and Agfa, with ISO ratings from 60 to 400. I've used most of the films currently available, and have taken pictures that I like with all of them. The only filters used are skylight and UV filters, and occasionally a polarizer.

However, more important than camera, lenses, films, or filters is the ability to see. The camera is only a tool used to take a photograph; the person behind it makes the picture. The camera is "an extension of your eye, nothing else," according to Ernst Haas. My aim in photography is to render objects in nature (with or without human elements) into pleasing or striking views. The effectiveness of the photographs lies in the handling of form, color, and composition, elements which are characteristic of all pictures. Another aim is to show some of the outstanding qualities of a chosen subject - in this case, the Adirondack Park - to a wider audience. For those who have been there, the photographs should be reminders of views already seen; for others, an encouragement to visit the area to see what it really looks like. In either case, the pictures should communicate my feeling that the Adirondack Region is a special place.

The one hundred photographs presented here were chosen from several thousand I've taken over the past few years. I have gained a greater knowledge and deeper appreciation of the Adirondacks in that time, and I've come to realize that there will always be new places to explore, as well as many more possibilities for pictures. I appreciate the Adirondacks more because of my photographic activities, and my photography has grown because I have found a subject which continually offers new personal and aesthetic challenges. I will be returning to the Adirondack Region often in the years to come - for recreation as well as photography.